Tim Dillon

Portraits of the USA

Fireworks, Washington, D.C., July 4, 1984

Space shuttle Atlantis, Cape Canaveral, Fla., Nov. 26, 1985.

Skate sailing, Lake Minnetonka, Minn., December 1982.

Acey Harper

Book design by Richard Curtis and Acey Harper

Published by
ACROPOLIS BOOKS, LTD.
Colortone Building, 2400 17th St., N.W.
Washington, D.C. 20009

Printed in the United States of America by
COLORTONE PRESS
Creative Graphics, Inc.
Washington, D.C. 20009

The Library of Congress Cataloging
in Publication Data
    Portraits of the USA
    Includes index.
    1. United States—Description and travel—
1981—Views.
I. USA TODAY (Arlington, Va.)
E169.04.P66 1986 973.92 86-8053
ISBN 0-87491-815-4

Portraits of the USA

Edited and designed by Acey Harper and Richard A. Curtis

ACROPOLIS BOOKS LTD.
WASHINGTON, D.C.

Twilight, Denver, January 1983.

About this book

Few things evoke such a range of emotions as the family photo album. It chronicles the people in our lives and marks the chapters of our lives.

These pages are just that, a scrapbook of the USA. Each photograph was selected because it captures and reflects something of the spirit of our nation — from the teacher in the one-room schoolhouse to the military widow at graveside to the superstar in performance.

The photographs speak of the warmth of peace and the scars of war. They tell of lessons learned from the past and of our dreams for the future. Come visit with us:

■ The children. Here you'll share the scariness of the first day of school. And the pride of a little Korean girl becoming a USA citizen.

■ The soldiers. The brave commemorating Vietnam — remembering and being remembered, finally tipping the scales of public concern. Then the wounded coming home from Beirut.

■ The famous. Entertainers whose music and humor enliven and enrich our lives. And athletes, whose victories and defeats we share.

As our journey winds, you'll also meet a pop conductor and a cattle rancher. A Nevada cowboy, and a Mississippi cotton grower whose body aches from working the land. And the homeless.

As we reacquaint ourselves with our Statue of Liberty, we honor the men and the women for whom she stands.

These are the portraits of the USA.

— John C. Quinn, Editor
USA TODAY

Crashing waves, San Francisco, Calif., January 1983.

Fresh faces

Each day is a new world for a child, whether it is the first day of school, the first steps toward a dream, or a new life in a new nation.

Above

Baltimore, Md., May 1983

A moment for Mother's Day — Christine Arrington and baby Prince Lee a day after he entered the world.

Photographer:
Barbara Ries

Right

Baltimore, Md., March 1983

A tiny hand, but a bigger story. Brendan Byrne weighed only 1 pound, 10 ounces when he was born three months premature in December 1982. Thanks to medical advances he grows to 3 pounds, 13 ounces, and would soon go home.

Photographer:
Barbara Ries

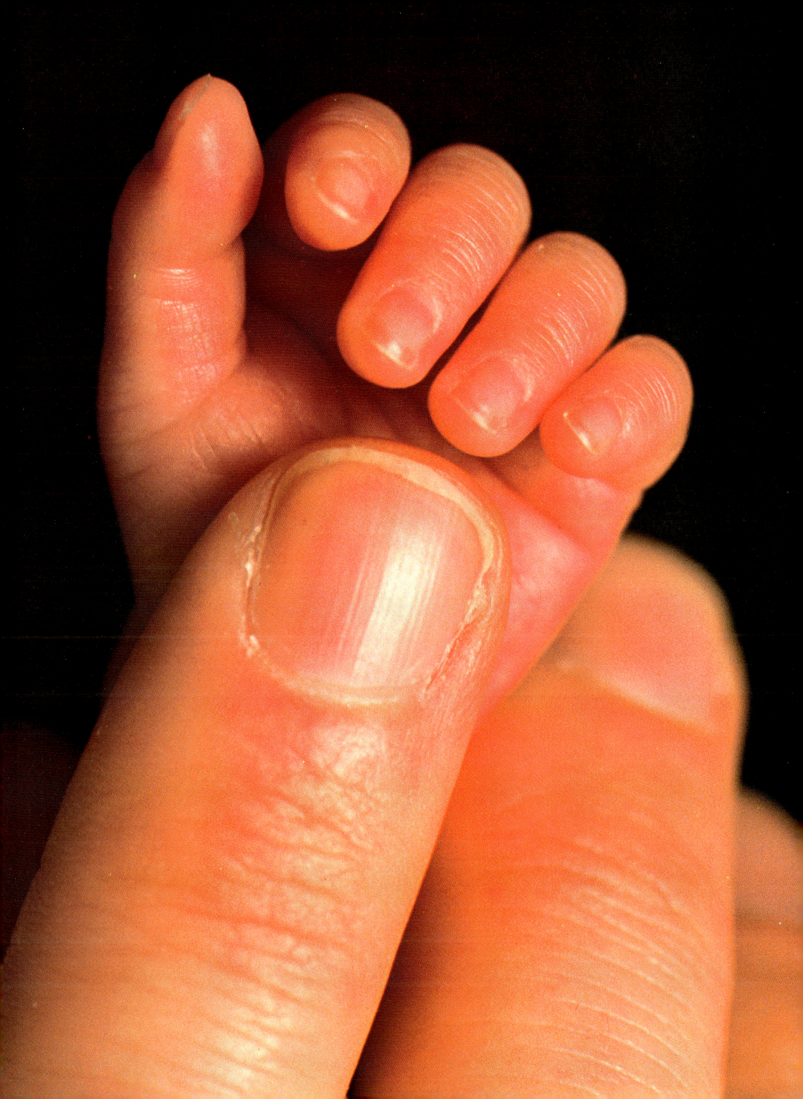

**Jacksonville, Fla.,
December 1984**

Facing life in the 80s, new
parents see things the
modern way. Robert and
Pamela Waldron already
have a savings account for
baby Lauren's college
education. And fathers are
more involved: "I think it's
important to share the
whole experience, even
when it means I don't get
eight hours sleep anymore,"
Robert says.

Photographer:
Acey Harper

Above

**Felicity, Ohio,
December 1982**

Family members defer to
Clyde Garrison, the
epitome of the family
patriarch. Everyone, that is,
except grandson Justin.
Cuddled in his granddad's
lap, he turns Garrison to
butter.

Photographer:
Acey Harper

Right

**Philadelphia, Pa.,
October 1983**

Two little girls, two purple
dresses, a few giggles and
some smiles. Photographed
on the doorstep of a
renovated rowhouse, sisters
Hilary and Courtney
Hansen said they felt like
fashion models.

Photographer:
Acey Harper

**Melville, N.Y.,
April 1984**

Some things never change,
like a child's dream. Here
JoAnne Murphy, who
would love to be in the
Olympics, nuzzles Megan,
after a riding lesson in the
New York countryside.

Photographer:
Barbara Ries

**Sagaponack, N.Y.,
May 1983**

The Sagaponack Common
School District is a one-
room schoolhouse built in
1885, and furnished with
old-fashioned wrought iron
desks. "Just the furniture is
dated," says teacher Regina
Guyer, "hopefully not our
methods." Teaching the
same children four years in
a row makes the classroom
"almost a family."

Photographer:
Robert Deutsch

**Powder Springs, Ga.,
August 1983**

New lunch boxes, new
dresses and new fears mark
the opening of Still
Elementary School for first
graders Katherine Ko,
Melissa McGee and Danica
Walker.

Photographer:
Barbara Ries

Left

**Washington, D.C.,
April 1985**

Going to the circus is a lot different when you're there with the President. The ever-present Secret Service agent sits directly behind President Reagan. Among the students from Martin Luther King Jr. Elementary School is Reagan's pen pal Rudolph Lee-Hines, at the president's left. The two shared popcorn.

Photographer:
Tim Dillon

Overleaf

**Union City, N.J.,
April 1983**

Union City is home to the USA's second-largest concentration of Marielitos — Cuban refugees who fled in the 1980 boatlift. And a bank parking lot is a baseball diamond to these children. After a game, they pause along a nearby wall.

Photographer:
Acey Harper

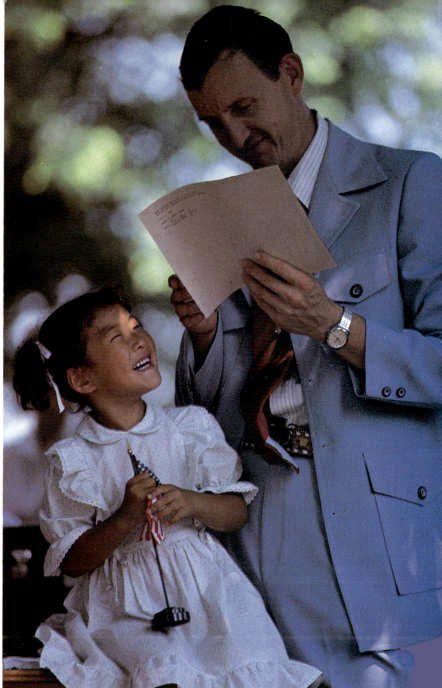

**Washington, D.C.,
July 1985**

Teen-ager Wendy Wang
from Brooklyn, N.Y., was
with her mother and
brother for a pro-Taiwan
demonstration when
China's President Li
Xiannian visited President
Reagan. Wendy holds flags
from her old nation and her
new one.

Photographer:
Barbara Ries

**Charlottesville, Va.,
July 1983**

Tonya Williams, a native
Korean, becomes a citizen
at an annual swearing-in
ceremony at Monticello,
Thomas Jefferson's estate.
Tonya, 4½ here, was
adopted by the Williams
family of Christiansburg,
Va., when she was 16
months old. Beaming is her
father, Kenneth.

Photographer:
Barbara Ries

Left

**St. Louis, Mo.,
May 1984**

Huong Thu Nguyen and
her daughter, Nga, 12 here,
came to St. Louis via a
special program bringing
Amerasian children to this
country. Huong raised her
child alone without the
serviceman father. She
found work in a linen
factory and calls herself
Rose. Nga goes by Nancy
and loves rock 'n' roll.

Photographer:
Acey Harper

Proudly we serve

The stories of USA servicemen are universal. A red heart gently pressed near a soldier's name at the Vietnam Veterans Memorial. A wobbly wave from a stretcher. A spontaneous burst of pride at the Naval Academy in Annapolis. On these 16 pages, a scrapbook of loss and reconciliation, homecoming and joy.

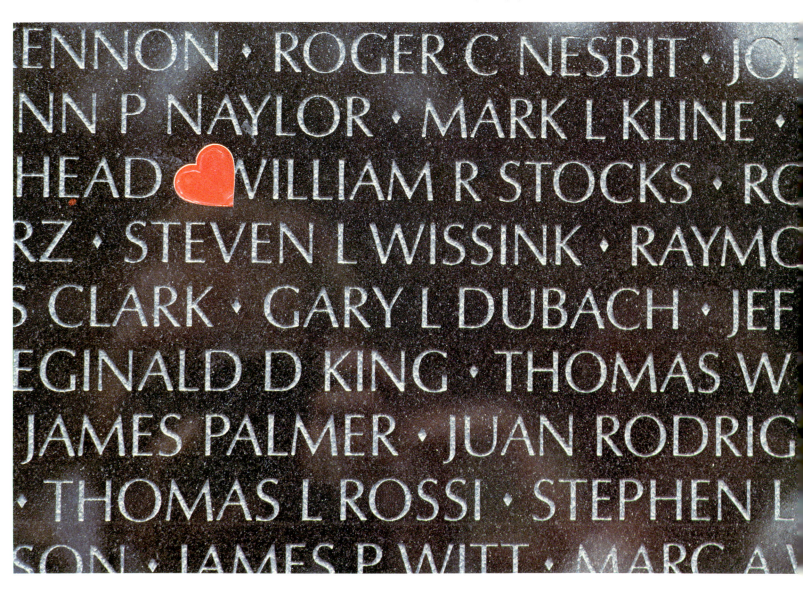

Left

Arlington, Va., May 1984

On an overcast day in May, the casket carrying the body of the Unknown Serviceman of the Vietnam Conflict finally is brought to a resting place at Arlington National Cemetery. As the casket team — representing each military branch — carry it, the only sound is the clicking of the soldiers' shoe taps on the stones.

Photographer:
David Hathcox

Above

Washington, D.C., November 1984

William Stock's mother, Eleanor Wimbish, writes letters to her son for every major holiday, on each anniversary of his death, Feb. 13, 1969, and "whenever I feel a need to get close to him." The letters are left on the ground below her son's name, one of about 58,000 names inscribed on the black granite wall of the Vietnam Veterans Memorial. This, she says, is how she copes.

Photographer:
Tim Dillon

Overleaf

Washington, D.C., May 1983

Charles Eatley, John Gallagher, Gregory Fulkerson and James Frisina cried when they heard "Taps" at the first Memorial Day service at the Vietnam Veterans Memorial. "We were all touching, thankful we're still here," Eatley says.

Fulkerson remembers feeling "very, very, very sad." Gallagher recalls that people came up and thanked him for serving in Vietnam. Frisina says he felt that finally, all his brother vets were home again.

Photographer:
Barbara Ries

Above

**Washington, D.C.,
November 1982**

A crowd of 150,000 listens to the dedication of the Vietnam Memorial on the Mall near the Lincoln Memorial. Some wave flags. Says Jan Scruggs, the Vietnam vet behind it all: "If I were a Vietnam veteran out of work...I'm not sure the memorial dedication would make me feel a heck of a lot better. But maybe a little better, knowing the names of my friends, my dead friends, are on the Mall."

Photographer:
Barbara Ries

Right

**New York, N.Y.,
May 1985**

Dennis Keating, hoists the stars and stripes high during a ticker-tape parade for Vietnam veterans. Marching in the parade, he says, was "a high that can never be matched."

Photographer:
Robert Deutsch

Above

Andrews Air Force Base, Md., April 1983

Seventeen USA citizens were killed in a terrorist bombing at the U.S. embassy in Beirut on April 18, 1983. At the grim homecoming where caskets were lined up, President Reagan told the bereaved: "We would indeed fail them if we let that act deter us from carrying on our mission."

Photographer:
Tim Dillon

Right

Andrews Air Force Base, Md., October 1983

Left to right: Lance Cpl. Burham Matthews, Lance Cpl. Michael Balcom and Lance Cpl. James Dudney arrive from the Marine headquarters bombing. Matthews is angry the USA did not avenge the attack, which prompted accusations the Marines were not properly protected. But if asked to go back, he would.

Photographer:
Tim Dillon

Following page

Andrews Air Force Base, Md., October 1983

Lance Cpl. Anthony Banks waves from the stretcher to "let them know I'm still here, I'm still with it." Banks came home alive from the Oct. 23 terrorist bombing in Beirut, Lebanon that killed 241 at Marine headquarters. The blast left Banks sightless in his right eye.

Photographer:
Tim Dillon

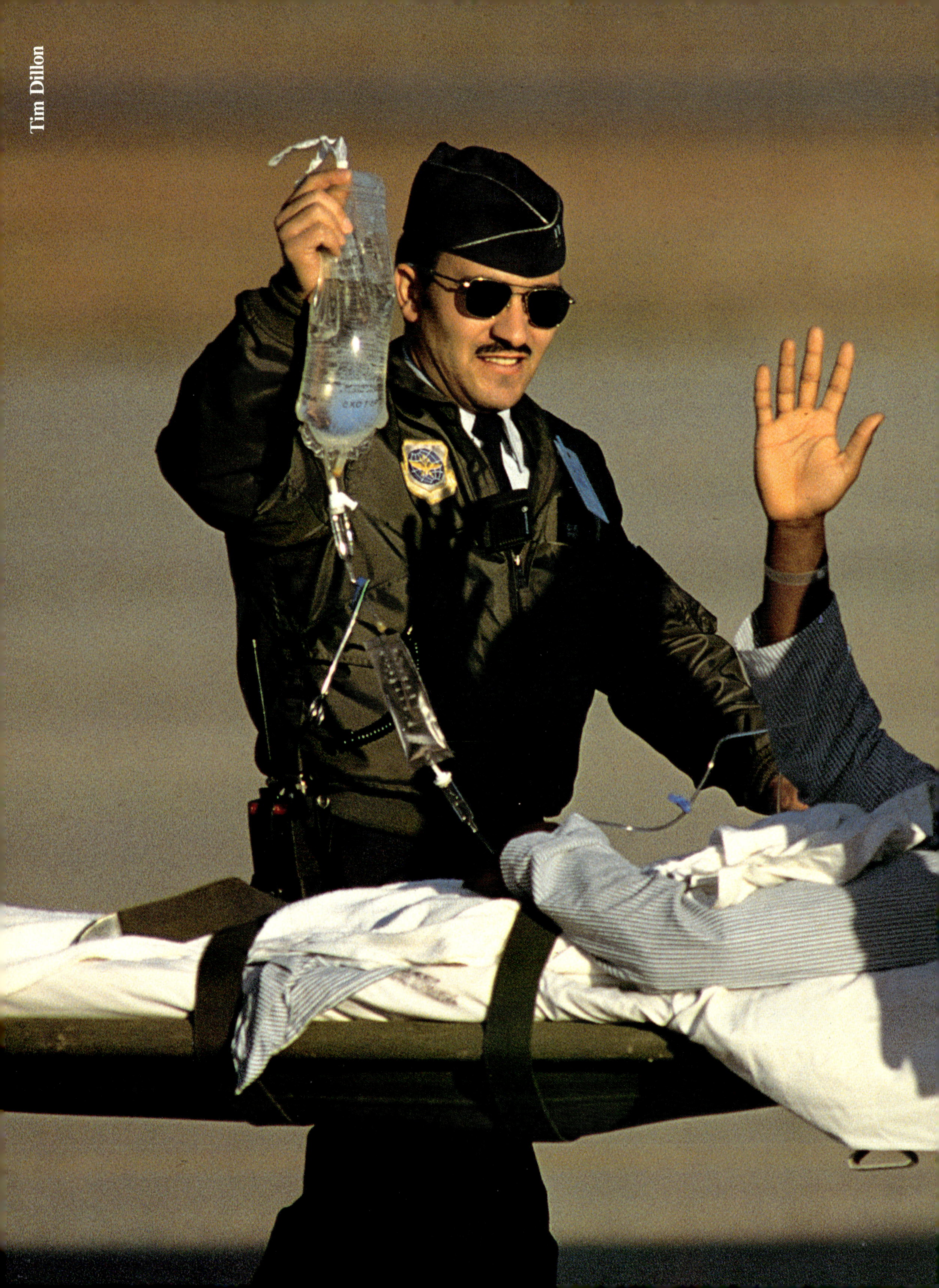

Tim Dillon

Tim Dillon

Preceding page

**Arlington, Va.,
October 1984**

"They really don't have any peace and I don't have a husband." — Debra Green, of Baltimore, Md., widow of Cpl. Davin Green, killed in the bombing of Marine headquarters in Beirut the year before.

Photographer:
Tim Dillon

Left

**Wayne, Pa.,
December 1982**

Roy Newman practices a sword and saber drill at Valley Forge Military Academy and Junior College. Attendance has increased steadily at the school in the past 20 years.

Photographer:
Acey Harper

Above

**Annapolis, Md.,
May 1983**

Midshipmen march in a formal dress parade during Commissioning Week at the U.S. Naval Academy in Annapolis.

Photographer:
H. Darr Beiser

Overleaf

**Annapolis, Md.,
May 1983**

The traditional hat toss climaxes Commissioning Week at the U.S. Naval Academy. Afterward, the graduates rarely bother to pick up the hats.

Photographer:
H. Darr Beiser

Bright lights

They entertain us; they fascinate us. They bring us joy; they make us smile and tap our feet. They release us from our cares. We demand that they not be just like us. Yet we dream of being them, of sharing in their glory.

Above

Champaign, Ill., September 1985

The first megaconcert to help debt-ridden farmers, Farm Aid stars 50 performers for 14 hours before 80,000 fans. Says organizer and country star Willie Nelson: "What we really want, through Farm Aid, is to change the attitude of the average person toward his ham and eggs in the morning."

Photographer:
Barbara Kinney

Right

Philadelphia, Pa., July 1985

The Live Aid concert — held simultaneously in Philadelphia and London — is the world's largest televised concert, drawing 1.5 billion TV viewers and pledges for famine victims in Africa. The steamy duet by Mick Jagger and Tina Turner is Live Aid's crowd teaser.

Photographer:
Barbara Kinney

Above and right

Washington, D.C., August 1985

Bruce Springsteen found Glory Days everywhere he took his "Born in the U.S.A. Tour." Above, he is welcomed home after touring abroad. The Boss frequently, and quietly, donates to charity, and occasionally performs benefits.

Photographer:
Barbara Kinney

Above

**New York, N.Y.,
January 1985**

Miles Davis is a jazz legend with an exquisite tone — a sound that fans immediately recognize. He's never been content to rest or repeat himself. A self-description of his music: "I play what I feel."

Photographer:
Robert Deutsch

Right

**Mt. Tamalpais, Calif.,
April 1985**

Guitarist Luther Tucker has picked with Chicago legends such as Muddy Waters and Sonny Boy Williamson.

Photographer:
Doug Menuez

Left

**Miami, Fla.,
January 1985**

With a hot soundtrack and cool attitudes, *Miami Vice*'s Don Johnson and Philip Michael Thomas have redefined cop shows for the MTV generation.

Photographer:
Acey Harper

Above

**White House, Tenn.,
December 1985**

"Ernest is either your brother-in-law or the guy who works on your car. Everyone can relate to him. He doesn't know he's irritating. There's no malice, really. He's just trying to help you out." — Actor Jim Varney, on alter-ego Ernest P. Worrell, the commercial success.

Photographer:
Barbara Ries

Overleaf

**New York, N.Y.,
February 1986**

"I hung around and I hung in there. It's like I always said, cream rises." — entertainer Pia Zadora. Her movies were flops, but her singing charmed critics in a 1986 concert tour.

Photographer:
Michael Keating

Left

**San Francisco, Calif.,
July 1985**

"I didn't start playing rock
'n' roll because I wanted to
be famous and I didn't start
because I wanted to get
girls. I started because I
wanted to be in a band." —
rocker Huey Lewis, of Huey
Lewis and the News.

Photographer:
Doug Menuez

Above

**New York, N.Y.,
September 1985**

"Bright, fun, beautiful and
crazy" is the way agent
Mort Viner describes long-
time client Shirley
MacLaine. Her best-selling
autobiographies — *Out on
a Limb* and *Dancing in the
Light* — chronicle her
beliefs in reincarnation and
her madcap love affairs.

Photographer:
Robert Deutsch

Above

Los Angeles, Calif., February 1985

Girls just wanna have fun! Campy rocker Cyndi Lauper gets a lift from pro wrestling buddy Hulk Hogan after she wins a Grammy as best new artist.

Photographer:
Barbara Kinney

Right

Los Angeles, Calif., October 1984

The A Team's Mr. T first grabbed headlines as Clubber Lang in *Rocky III.* "I didn't have to act. I've been Clubber all my life. He's mean and hungry just like me."

Photographer:
Bob Riha Jr.

Top of the roster

Sports at their best are more than mere games. We see sacrifice, extraordinary effort, heroes, the defeated. The sports are as different as the faces, but one thing is the same — the drive to excel.

Above

New York, N.Y., April 1985

The battle for the Big Apple begins. Though the Yankees would fire Yogi Berra before season's end, and Dave Johnson's Mets would fall short of a pennant, the two teams fought fiercely for fans and fame.

Photographer:
Acey Harper

Right

Claremont, S.D., August 1985

Baseball blossoms in towns across the USA. The Claremont Honkers won the 1985 state Amateur Baseball Class B championship. Claremont Honkers pausing in a sunflower field, clockwise from top: Tom Pahl, Sherm Cutler, Mike Cutler and Harold Feser.

Photographer:
Mitch Kezar

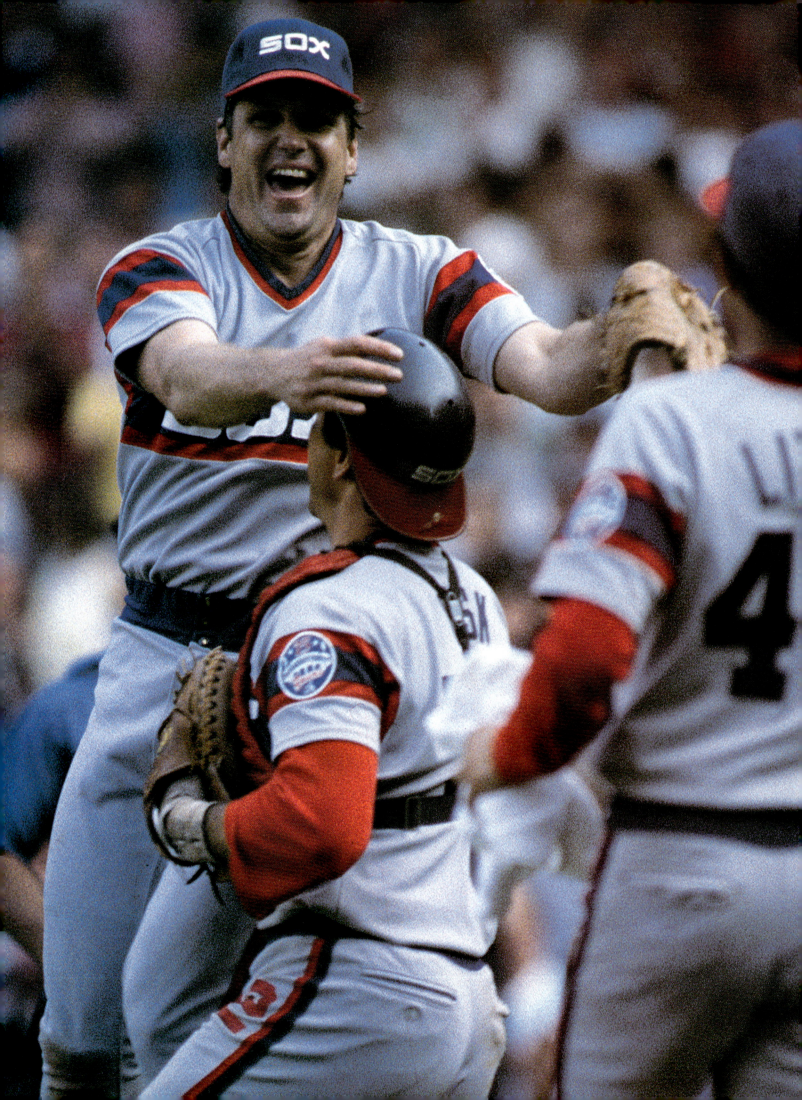

Left

**New York, N.Y.,
August 1985**

Tom Seaver wins his 300th
game in New York —
where he first gained fame
with the Mets. At 41, and
here with the Chicago
White Sox, he proves he is
still Tom Terrific.

Photographer:
Robert Deutsch

Above

**New York, N.Y.,
April 1985**

In one of their last
moments together at the
Yankee Stadium they ruled
in the '60s, home-run
legends Mickey Mantle and
Roger Maris clown for fans.
Maris died eight months
later.

Photographer:
Robert Deutsch

Overleaf

**Chicago, Ill.,
October 1984**

The National Football
League's all-time leading
rusher, Chicago Bears'
Walter Payton leaves a
tackler grabbing at air. "I'm
not here to change history,"
he says, "I'm here to play
football."

Photographer:
Richard Derk

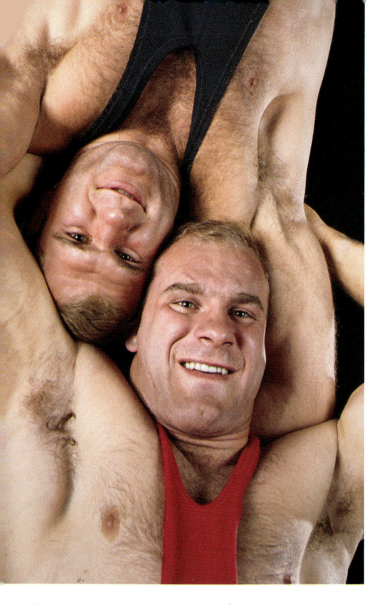

Above

**Allendale, Mich.,
June 1984**

Twins Lou, bottom, and Ed Banach took their freestyle wrestling techniques to the Olympics where they both won golds. After successful college careers, Ed became assistant coach at Iowa State University and Lou at the U.S. Military Academy at West Point.

Photographer:
Tim Dillon

Right

**Las Vegas, Nev.,
September 1983**

Already knocked down once by Aaron Pryor, former champion Alexis Arguello stays down for the night, but later continued to try reviving his career.

Photographer:
John T. Barr

**San Francisco, Calif.,
April 1984**

"I didn't start anything aerobic until I was 48," says Sister Marion Irvine. At 54 years old, she was the oldest woman to participate in the marathon trials for the 1984 Summer Olympics.

Photographer:
Doug Menuez

**Atlanta, Ga.,
July 1985**

A cool end to a hot race. Misty spray from fire hydrants refreshes runners just completing the annual July 4 10-kilometer Peachtree Road Race.

Photographer:
Charlie Archambault

Left

**New York, N.Y.,
September 1985**

Tennis pro Pam Shriver
plays in the shadow of
Martina Navratilova and
Chris Evert Lloyd. Yet she
still aspires to No. 1: "I feel
good about tennis," she
says. "I feel I'm still
improving."

Photographer:
Barbara Kinney

Above

**Augusta, Ga.,
April 1984**

A day before facing the
pressure of The Masters,
superstar pro golfer Tom
Watson shares the beauty of
the Augusta National
course with daughter, Meg,
then 4.

Photographer:
Porter Binks

Overleaf

**Carlsbad, Calif.,
January 1986**

"Just another one of the
tricks we do," says top
professional motocross rider
Ron Lechien, of his
airborne antics.

Photographer:
Robert Beck

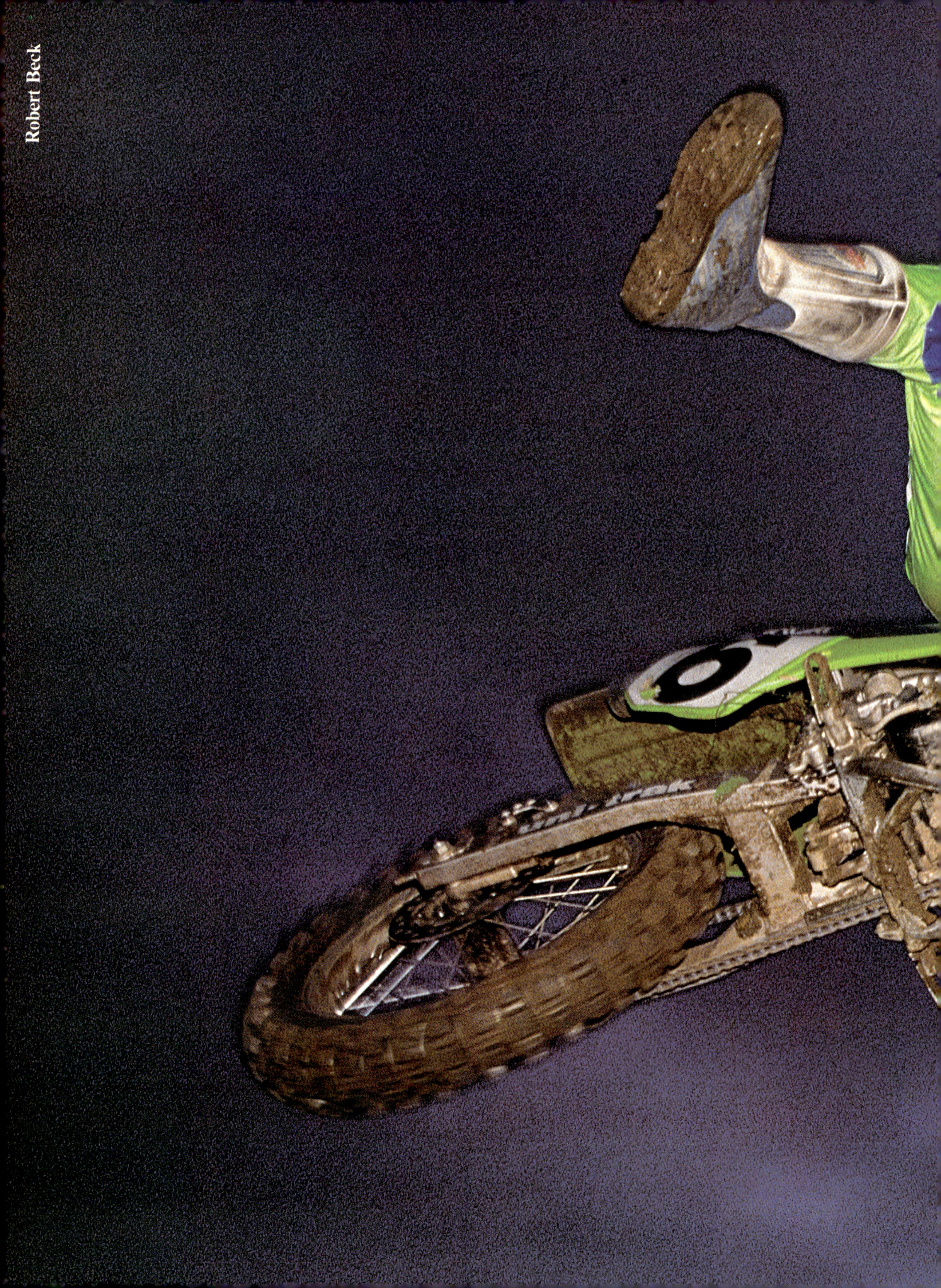

Robert Beck

Left

**St. Louis, Mo.,
March 1984**

Joey Meyer watches in disbelief as DePaul University loses the National Collegiate Athletic Association tournament game that ended his father's 42-year career as head coach. Father Ray watches over then-assistant Joey's shoulder. The next season, Joey took over.

Photographer:
Porter Binks

Above

**Durham, N.C.,
March 1986**

North Carolina's Kevin Madden, right, and Duke's Mark Alarie, reach for the ball in a battle between teams that were No. 1 in the USA during the season. Duke finished No. 2.

Photographer:
Porter Binks

Overleaf

**San Francisco, Calif.,
January 1985**

Thor Stone took off in martial arts at age 2, earning a second degree black belt in karate at age 8. He's 11 here.

Photographer:
Doug Menuez

**Plantation Key, Fla.,
February 1984**

Windsurfing rides a wave of
popularity, with 72,000
sailboards sold in 1985. For
sports enthusiasts who love
water and winter skiers
looking for a summer
substitute, windsurfing
picked up steam when it
was introduced in the 1984
Summer Olympics.

Photographer:
Jeffrey Cardenas

Above

**Los Angeles, Calif.,
July 1984**

Let the Games begin! Jesse
Owens' granddaughter Gina
Hemphill carries his legacy
— and the Olympic torch
— into the L.A. Memorial
Coliseum for the opening of
the 1984 Summer
Olympics.

Photographer:
H. Darr Beiser

Right

**Los Angeles, Calif.,
July 1984**

The spectacular opening of
the 1984 Summer Games
rivals a Cecil B. DeMille
movie. With a Soviet
boycott the USA would
grab 174 medals — 83 of
them gold — in its best
haul ever.

Photographer:
Jeffrey Cardenas

Left

**Los Angeles, Calif.,
August 1984**

Carl Lewis takes the USA's
4 x -100-meter relay team to
victory, completing the
Olympic odyssey that
brought him an
extraordinary four gold
medals.

Photographer:
H. Darr Beiser

Above

**Los Angeles, Calif.,
August 1984**

The long ride for one-time
Harlem bike messenger
Nelson Vails, left, ends with
him embracing USA
teammate Mark Gorski.
Gorski, training since he
was 14, won the sprint
cycling gold, Vails the
silver, Japan's Tsutomu
Sakamoto the bronze.

Photographer:
H. Darr Beiser

Left

**Los Angeles, Calif.,
August 1984**

Tracie Ruiz and Candy
Costie made a worldwide
splash with their gold
medals in synchronized
swimming, which debuted
as an Olympic sport.

Photographer:
Gary Voth

Above

**Los Angeles, Calif.,
August 1984**

Dwight Stones doesn't earn
a medal but does win
cheers in his hometown
after placing fourth in the
high jump.

Photographer:
H. Darr Beiser

Left	*Above*	*Overleaf*
Los Angeles, Calif., August 1984	**Los Angeles, Calif., August 1984**	**Lake Casitas, Calif., July 1984**
Greg Louganis dives to gold medals in platform and springboard events. His record score makes him the best Olympic diver of the modern era.	Joan Benoit Samuelson relishes the moment after easily winning the first women's Olympic marathon. "It was like following the Yellow Brick Road."	Kayakers carry paddles in the quiet dawn.
Photographer: **Gary Voth**	*Photographer:* **H. Darr Beiser**	*Photographer:* **Porter Binks**

Left

**Los Angeles, Calif.,
August 1984**

A defeated Mary. Mary Decker Slaney cries after her dramatic fall in the women's 3000-meters, the Games' most controversial moment. Decker blamed Britain's Zola Budd for the collision, then defeated Budd in a 1985 rematch in London.

Photographer:
Gary Voth

Above

**Los Angeles, Calif.,
August 1984**

The winningest Mary. A perfect 10 netted the 4-10 Olympic sweetheart, Mary Lou Retton, the gold medal in all-around gymnastics competition. Retton would later become the biggest commercial winner of the Games.

Photographer:
Kathleen Hennessy

Give me shelter

How many homeless are there? No one can say for sure. The government says there are 250,000 to 350,000; other groups say there are as many as 3 million. Where will they sleep tonight?

Left

Washington, D.C., June 1985

"I strongly encourage people to reach out to the next person . . . who is desperate and homeless."

— Activist Mitch Snyder, whose 51-day fast inspired a film about the homeless.

Photographer:
Paul Fetters

Above

Philadelphia, Pa., December 1983

Clifford Chester fights chill while waiting for a shelter for the homeless to open.

Photographer:
Steve Falk

Lost amid the plenty

In March 1984, photographer Barbara Ries visited pockets of poverty in Belfast, Maine and Edwards, Miss. Meet two families: the Prentices and the Smiths.

Photo essay:
Barbara Ries

Left

Edwards, Miss., March 1984

Zachary Wolfe eats stew of beans and raccoon meat. When photographed, Zachary was temporarily living with his grandmother, Marzenna Smith.

Above

Edwards, Miss., March 1984

Marzenna Smith, and grandchildren Christopher, Sandra, Herbert and Zachary. Smith has lived in Edwards since 1938 and prepared her land by hand for cotton, corn and peanuts. As she grew older her muscles weakened and she has high blood pressure. "Some days I'm good and I do try to stay on my feet as best I can."

Overleaf

Belfast, Maine, March 1984

Cora Prentice hugs her father, Harold. "Cora does that to me all the time," says the father.

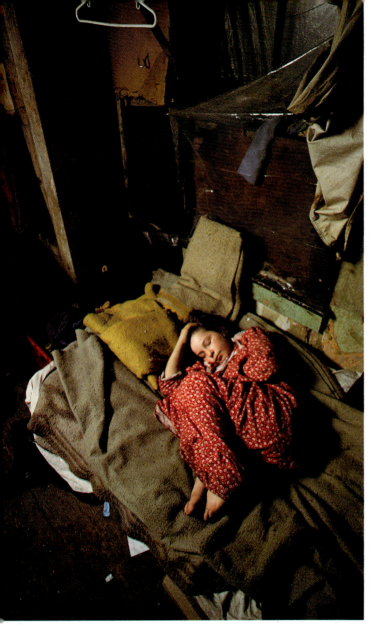

Above

**Belfast, Maine,
March 1984**

Cora Prentice curls up in a corner of the family's two-room tarpaper shack that has no indoor plumbing.

Right

**Belfast, Maine,
March 1984**

Alice Prentice helps daughter, Cora, with her homework. "We're just barely making it by the skin of our teeth," Prentice says. "And sometimes we're not doing that. . . I'd like to get oranges for her (Cora) but I can't afford it."

Omens of plague

AIDS, Acquired Immune Deficiency Syndrome, has gripped the nation this decade, claiming the lives of more than half its victims.

Above

Dayton, Ohio, December 1985

Rick Cecil, who works for a law firm, lost his lover to AIDS in October 1985. Cecil, stunned when he learned he himself has AIDS Related Complex (ARC), says "If I sneeze wrong, I think about it." Cecil considers himself one of the few lucky ones who has the support of family and friends.

Photographer:
Bruce Zake

Right

Salt Lake City, Utah, December 1985

AIDS victim Sheldon Spears feels this photo of himself "probably helps other people understand the loneliness that goes with the disease; the isolation." He founded the Utah AIDS Project.

Photographer:
Doug Menuez

The ageless

The nation is growing older, as the median age increases each year. For many, age brings only more yesterdays, for others more pain, and for most, more wisdom.

Above

Keams Canyon, Ariz., February 1985

Winter '85 was brutal in Arizona. Navajos such as Lois James, 86 here, were isolated when snow and ice left roads to their reservation impassable. James, who suffered strep throat, was flown out.

Photographer:
Doug Menuez

Right

Washington, D.C., April 1983

Lazar Schachter of Memphis, Tenn., carried this 1946 photo of himself to a convention of Holocaust survivors, hoping someone might recognize him. "I met a lot of people I hadn't seen in a long time," says the former Czechoslovakian. He has been in the USA since 1950.

Photographer:
Barbara Ries

Barbara Ries

Preceding page

**Brooklyn, N.Y.,
February 1983**

An old woman negotiates a
snow-covered street.

Photographer:
Barbara Ries

Above

**Tarboro, N.C.,
November 1983**

Identical twins George, left,
and Joe Grayiel, 65 here,
were best friends. They
dressed alike, buying
duplicates for each other.
"Anything Joe had was
mine," says George, "and
what I had was his."
George filled in on one of
Joe's dates, and ended up
marrying her. Joe died in
June 1985.

Photographer:
Acey Harper

Right

**Cherokee, N.C.,
March 1984**

"All of us full-blood
Cherokees, we're just about
all gone," says Albert
Crowe, with his wife of
more than 50 years, Regina.
He remembers having his
mouth washed out with
soap for speaking Cherokee
at public school in the early
1900s.

Photographer:
Barbara Ries

**Salem, W.Va.,
October 1984**

Autumn days are wonder days
With colors red and gold,
Summer is gone; fall is here
And the year is growing old.

And often do I like to think
That God, with mystic hand,
Has reached down from Heaven
And painted all the land.

— Poem by retired U.S. Sen. Jennings Randolph, D-W.Va., photographed in his hometown.

Photographer:
Barbara Ries

The Workers

They are the heartbeat of the USA. Their days may begin before dawn, and end after dark. Work may take them across the USA, or they may never leave town.

Left

Gloucester, Mass., October 1984

Capt. Cecilio Cecilio and his crew bring in their perch catch. From left, Jerry Royster, Paul Beal, Manuel Carrapichosi, Manuel Garcia and John Reboca. Cecilio sees his business dwindling since a 1984 World Court decision restricting USA fishing grounds. "We're not making the money we used to. Now we're boxed in."

Photographer:
Acey Harper

Above

Boothbay Harbor, Maine, July 1985

On a busy summer day, Becky Reed and other waitresses serve an average of 600 people up to 350 pounds of lobsters dripping in butter. About 45 percent of the nation's lobsters come from Maine. Diners take note: the female lobster is better, since it has more meat, less shell.

Photographer:
H. Darr Beiser

Overleaf

Brownsville, Texas, June 1983

A migrant worker picks okra on a Brownsville farm.

Photographer:
H. Darr Beiser

Left

Dunkerton, Iowa, October 1984

Ken Fettkether calls the movie *Country*, filmed on his farm in 1983, "right on target. Timing was perfect. Things haven't changed a bit, in fact they're getting worse." Fettkether, farming since 1955, says he'll continue, although the number of farm foreclosures and bankruptcies are the highest since the 1930s. "You keep hoping that something will arrive to make things look better."

Photographer:
Dixie D. Vereen

Above

Chillicothe, Texas, June 1984

From dawn 'til midnight, each June to November, about 3,000 crews of harvest workers with combines follow the ripening wheat. The annual migration from Texas to Canada means 15-hour days, lonely hauls on country roads and card games when it rains.

Photographer:
Zigy Kaluzny

Overleaf

Hope Mills, N.C., February 1985

"Anything that keeps you worried to death day to day isn't right," tobacco farmer Annie Mae Chavis says. She worries about the government controls limiting the number of tobacco farmers and how much they grow.

Photographer:
Dixie D. Vereen

Preceding page

**Arthur, Neb.,
August 1983**

Rancher Cecil Valentine, 68 here, lives within six miles of his birthplace on land that his "daddy-in-law" homesteaded. "I couldn't live in a city. They couldn't give me California."

Photographer:
H. Darr Beiser

Above

**Kissimmee, Fla.,
February 1983**

It was wet and cold the day Bar 7 Ranch manager John Clark rescued this calf. Heavy rains flooded Sturm Island, where Clark's cattle graze. Clark and neighbors used airboats and helicopters to drive about 200 head of cattle to the mainland. "My wife and I just about drowned in that lake that day."

Photographer:
Acey Harper

Right

**Keams Canyon, Ariz.,
February 1985**

Warm weather rapidly melted the heavy snows on the Navajo reservation, cutting off access roads. Bah Begay Cepi, 78 here, kept this lamb in her house, away from the cold mud.

Photographer:
Doug Menuez

Left

**Albany, Texas,
May 1984**

Watt Matthews, 85 here, has been a Texas rancher all his life. He raises cattle and some crops and has more than 100 working oil wells. He restored his 1856 ranch house stone by stone, "because my mother lived there as a child."

Photographer:
Zigy Kaluzny

Above

**Jiggs, Nev.,
January 1986**

Waddie Mitchell is a cowboy — and more. Among the cowboy poets gaining increasing attention, he thinks up rhymes as he rounds up cattle.

The clippity clop often fits the poetic meter. "It'd be hard for a lot of people to picture John Wayne up there goin' 'Roses are red, violets are purple,' " he says.

Overleaf

**Devil's Garden, Calif.,
March 1983**

Four times a year cowboys round up wild horses for the federal government's adopt-a-horse program. For $125, new owners get title after properly caring for the horse for a year. But the number available has been dropping.

Photographer:
John T. Barr

**Roseburg, Ore.,
November 1982**

Harley Campbell is scaling the deck. That's the lumberman's lingo for measuring logs to see how many board feet of plywood they'll produce.

Photographer:
Acey Harper

Anything goes

Some are whimsical, some are mystical. Still, the following photographs say the same thing: this is a nation where the unusual has a place, too.

Left

Independence, Mo., June 1985

Celebrating the old-fashioned way, Amy Brown, and brother, Gary, get ready for July 4 in Independence, the hometown and burial place of Harry S Truman.

Photographer:
Barbara Ries

Above

Toothachers Cove, Maine, April 1985

Music's magical maestro spins a treble clef. Erich Kunzel is the well-known conductor of pops concerts in Cincinnati and other cities.

Photographer:
Acey Harper

Overleaf

San Francisco, Calif., May 1985

Here's a sports event, San Francisco style — the Bay to Breakers run. The largest foot race in the USA, the 7½-mile course also attracts some of the zaniest runners in the nation.

Photographer:
Doug Menuez

Following pages

Cape May, N.J., July 1983

Shark fishing is big-game hunting on the water. Anglers, some of whom are attracted by the thrill of fighting Jaws, can struggle up to several hours to bag the brutes.

Photographer:
Paul Fetters

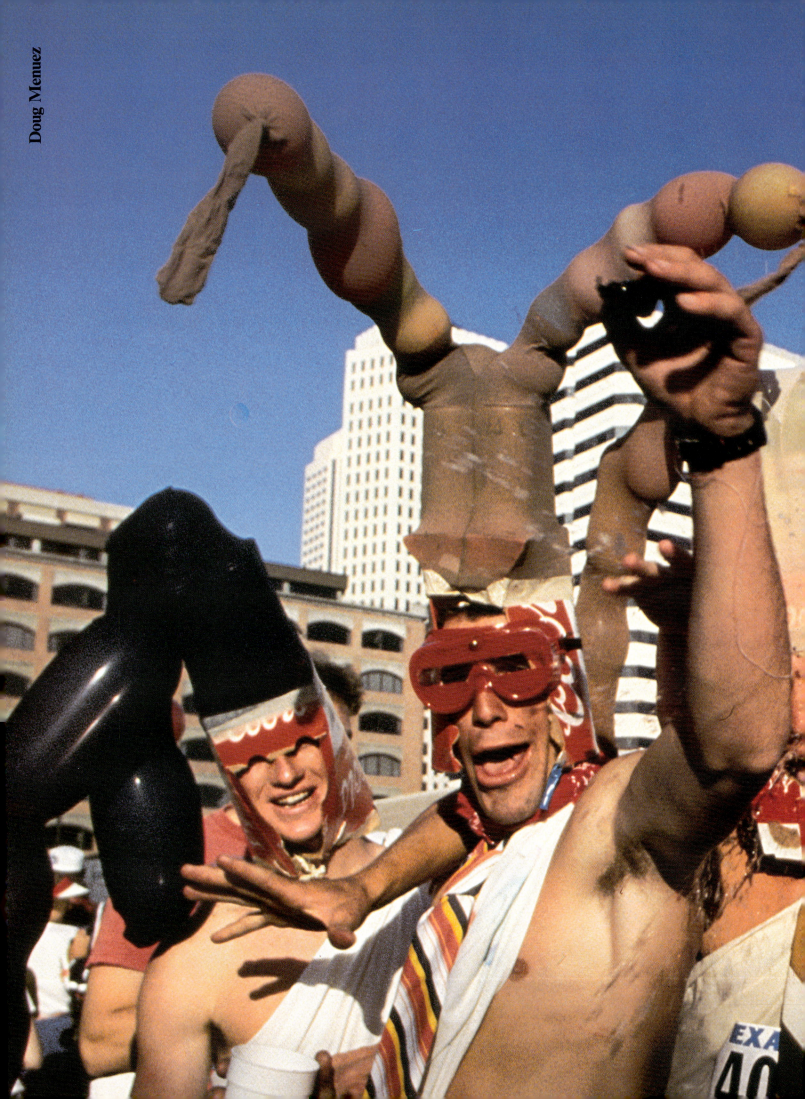

**Leominster, Mass.,
September 1985**

Don Featherstone is
responsible for these things.
He sculpted the original
flamingo lawn ornament in
1959 and now sells them.

Photographer:
Acey Harper

**New Orleans, La.,
March 1984**

His "fancy imagination"
inspires Blaine Kern to
build floats for the Mardi
Gras. Kern's company
provides everything from
doubloons thrown during
parades to celebrity
bookings for masquerade
balls.

Photographer:
Lee Crum

About the photographers

Edited and designed by Acey Harper and Richard A. Curtis

Mark Angeles

*Staff photographer,
Gannett News Service,
Washington, D.C.*

Angeles graduated from George Washington University in 1978. He has been a photographer with Gannett News Service since 1979 and helped with starting *Florida Today*, the new state-wide daily newspaper.

Charlie Archambault

*Freelancer,
Washington, D.C.*

Archambault became interested in photography while attending Emory and Henry College in Emory, Va. He continued his photo studies at Randolph Technical College in Asheboro, N.C., while working on small daily newspapers. Archambault freelanced in Atlanta for about 1½ years, before moving to Washington in 1985.

John T. Barr

*Freelancer,
Los Angeles, Calif.*

Barr began his newspaper career at age 16 as a stringer for United Press International in Pittsburgh. A 1972 graduate of Rochester Institute Of Technology, Barr worked for newspapers in Pennsylvania and New York before moving to Los Angeles in 1973. He worked as staff photographer for UPI then joined Gamma-Liaison, an international photo news agency. A photographer for *USA TODAY* from 1983 to 1985, Barr's work has appeared in *Time, Newsweek, Los Angeles Times,* and other publications.

Robert Beck

*Freelancer,
San Diego, Calif.*

Beck was a high school history and social studies teacher in Los Angeles when he took up photography to supplement his income. He moved to San Diego in 1984 to work at photography full time. As a surfer, Beck's work has appeared in surfing and sports magazines all over the world.

H. Darr Beiser

*Photo editor/photographer,
USA TODAY*

Beiser received his B.A. in journalism in 1976 at the University of Arizona in Tucson. He worked at the *Tucson Citizen* from 1977-1982 and joined *USA TODAY* as one of the newspaper's original staff photographers.

Porter Binks

*Sports picture editor,
USA TODAY*

Binks has a B.S. in criminal justice from the University of Tennessee at Chattanooga. He worked for the Tennessee Department of Safety and *The Chattanooga Times*, before moving to Washington, D.C. in 1982 to become a photo editor for The Associated Press. Binks joined *USA TODAY* in 1983.

Jeffrey Cardenas

*Freelancer,
Key West, Fla.*

A 1983 graduate of the University of Florida in Gainesville, Cardenas' photos have appeared in *The New York Times, The Boston Globe* and *Sports Illustrated.* In 1985 Cardenas was awarded a grant from the state of Florida to photograph underwater landscapes in the Florida Keys.

Lee Crum

*Freelancer,
New Orleans, La.*

A self-taught photographer, Crum has worked at the *Arkansas Democrat* in Little Rock, *The Times-Picayune/The States-Item* in New Orleans and *The Anchorage Times* in Alaska. He now specializes in portrait and advertising photography.

Malcolm Denemark

*Staff photographer,
Florida Today,
Cocoa, Fla.*

Denemark served in the Army, traveled to India and Nepal and owned a landscaping business before taking up photography. He has photography degrees from Brevard Community College in Cocoa, Fla. He has won prizes for news and feature photography from the Orlando Press Club. His work has appeared in *Life, Time, Newsweek* and *People.*

Richard Derk

*Freelancer,
Chicago, Ill.*

Derk became involved in photography while working on the student newspaper at the University of Illinois At Chicago where he was studying finance. He has worked as a photographer for the *Rockford (Ill.) Register Star* and various Chicago papers, including the *Sun-Times.* He has been a freelancer since 1984.

Robert Deutsch

*Staff photographer,
USA TODAY*

Deutsch graduated in 1971 from City College of New York, with a degree in physics, but his real love was photography. He tried studio photography in the New York City area then switched to news photography working for the Gannett newspapers in Westchester and Rockland counties. Deutsch joined the *USA TODAY* staff in 1984.

Tim Dillon

*Staff photographer,
USA TODAY*

A Washington, D.C., native, Dillon served as base newspaper editor in the Air Force at Langley Air Force Base, Va., and later attended the University of Maryland. He freelanced for *The Washington Star* and joined the *USA TODAY* staff in January 1986.

Steve Falk

*Freelancer,
Philadelphia, Pa.*

Falk is a contributing photographer for Gamma-Liaison, an international photo news agency, as well as a freelancer for *USA TODAY, The Philadelphia Inquirer* and The Associated Press. His work frequently appears in *Time, Newsweek, US News & World Report* and *The New York Times.*

Paul Fetters

Freelancer,
Washington, D.C.

Fetters attended Michigan State University on a swimming scholarship but got hooked on photography in his senior year. He studied photojournalism at the University of Missouri-Columbia, and has freelanced for *Forbes* and other magazines.

David Hathcox

Freelancer,
Washington, D.C.

Hathcox earned a master's degree at East Texas State University at Texarkana. He was a staff photographer at *The Paris* (Texas) *News*, then was chief photographer at *The Laredo* (Texas) *Times* from 1977-80. He has freelanced in Washington, D.C., since 1980.

Acey Harper

Photo editor/photographer,
USA TODAY

Harper, one of the designers of *Portraits of the USA*, started out as a copy boy at the *The Palm Beach* (Fla.) *Post-Evening Times*, where he became interested in photography. He graduated from the University of Florida in Gainesville and worked at the *Fort Myers News-Press*, before joining *USA TODAY* at its inception in 1982.

Kathleen Hennessy

Lab director,
USA TODAY

Hennessy was intrigued by photography as a child — her best friend's father was a professional photographer and Hennessy found his studio fascinating. She graduated from the Arizona State University in Tempe then went to work at a commercial photography studio in Scottsdale, Ariz., before moving to Washington, D.C. She joined *USA TODAY* in September 1983.

Zigy Kaluzny

Freelancer,
Austin, Texas

Kaluzny has a master's in classical archaeology from the University Of Chicago. His work appears regularly in *Time, Newsweek, Geo, Stern, Der Spiegel, The New York Times* as well as *USA TODAY.*

Michael Keating

Staff photographer,
The Cincinnati Enquirer

Michael Keating has been a staff photographer for *The Cincinnati Enquirer* since 1978. Prior to that he was a staff photographer for *The Evansville* (Ind.) *Courier* and *The Evansville Press*. He was named Indiana Photographer of the Year in 1977.

Mitch Kezar

Freelancer,
Minneapolis, Minn.

Kezar was formerly the director of photography at the *Tampa* (Fla.) *Tribune*, a picture editor at the *Minneapolis Star and Tribune* and a staff photographer for *The Alabama Journal and Advertiser* in Montgomery. His works appear in corporate communications, annual reports and many national publications, such as *National Geographic, Business Week, Life, Forbes* and *Fortune.*

Barbara Kinney

Photo editor/photographer,
USA TODAY

Kinney graduated from the University of Kansas in 1980 and moved to Washington, D.C., soon after. She worked for a trade association magazine and did freelance photography before joining *USA TODAY* in 1982.

Doug Menuez

Contract photographer,
USA TODAY,
San Francisco, Calif.

At age 10, Menuez began taking pictures with his father's camera. As a teen-ager he couldn't decide whether to pursue music or photography as a career but ended up earning a degree in photojournalism at San Francisco State University. He started shooting for *USA TODAY* in 1982.

Barbara Ries

Staff photographer,
USA TODAY

Ries graduated in 1980 from the University of Missouri-Columbia School of Journalism. Before joining the *USA TODAY* staff in 1983, Ries worked in Washington, D.C., as a freelancer for *The Washington Star*, United Press International and *The Philadelphia Inquirer.*

Bob Riha Jr.

Contract photogapher,
USA TODAY,
Los Angeles, Calif.

A freelancer for *USA TODAY* since 1983, Riha has freelanced for The Associated Press, United Press International, the *Los Angeles Times* and the Long Beach, Calif., *Press-Telegram.*

Dixie D. Vereen

Photo editor/photographer,
USA TODAY

Vereen first tried photography when she worked for her high school newspaper and annual. She received a degree in photojournalism from Randolph Technical College, Asheboro, N.C. Before joining *USA TODAY* in 1982, Vereen worked at a number of newspapers including *The Raleigh* (N.C.) *Times* and *The* (Raleigh) *News & Observer, Newsday* and *The Philadelphia Inquirer.*

Gary Voth

Staff photographer,
The Sun,
San Bernardino, Calif.

Voth studied communications and photography at Chaffey Community College, Alta Loma, Calif. When not making pictures, Voth writes software for Apple computers.

Bruce Zake

Freelancer,
Columbus, Ohio

A 1982 journalism graduate of Ohio University in Athens, Zake has worked for *The News Herald* in Willoughby, Ohio, and freelanced in Tampa, Fla., before moving to Columbus, Ohio.

A note of thanks

There are dozens of USA TODAY staff members, besides those listed above, who gave time and effort to make this book a reality. We can't list them all but a few deserve special mention. We would especially like to thank Tony Casale who coordinated this project, Jan Perna who researched and wrote the captions. Also thanks to Amy Eisman for editing those captions.

Also thanks to: Marsha Hayden, Arabella Stewart-Stern, J. Taylor Buckley Jr., Darcy Trick, Tom Weir, Larry Nylund, George Edmonson, Kitty Yancey, Paul White, Jeffrey L. Albert and, at Acropolis Books, Robert Hickey.

Finally, a special mention for Allen H. Neuharth, the founder of USA TODAY and John C. Quinn, the editor. Without their vision neither the newspaper nor this book would have been possible.

— **Nancy J. Woodhull,**
Senior Editor

Lincoln Memorial, Washington, D.C., February 1986.